MEMORY WORKOUT

Jonathan Hancock

Illustrated by Sean Longcroft

Hodder Children's Books

a division of Hodder Headline plc

For Lucy.

Published by Hodder Children's Books 1999

'Activator' is a registered trade mark owned by and used with the permission of Addison Wesley Longman Limited.

Edited by Jacqueline Dineen
Series designed by Fiona Webb
Book designed by Joy Mutter

10 9 8 7 6 5 4 3 2 1

A catalogue record for this book is available from the British Library.

ISBN: 0 340 736267

Printed by Clays Ltd, St Ives plc.

Hodder Children's Books
a division of Hodder Headline plc
338 Euston Road
London NW1 3BH

Meet the author

Jonathan Hancock had a good reason to develop a phenomenal memory; he wanted to win a bet. He was challenged by some friends to try to get into *The Guinness Book of Records* and was looking for something he could attempt, when one particular listing caught his eye. On a television programme in Japan, someone had shuffled six packs of playing cards then memorised them all, one by one. Jonathan had always been interested in magic tricks with cards and it occurred to him that there might be some trick to remembering cards too. He decided to experiment.

Six months later, Jonathan broke the world record and won a place in *The Guinness Book of Records*. He won the World Student Memory Championship and then achieved the ultimate title – World Memory Champion – breaking several more records along the way. He has since written four books about memory, appeared on many different television and radio programmes, and now works in schools and businesses to help people who want to make the most of their brains.

So what's his secret? What was the trick Jonathan Hancock discovered that won him the bet and allowed him to develop the best memory in the world?

You're about to find out!

Introduction

Learning to remember changed my life. I used to have a pretty good memory but nothing special. Now I never forget anything.

As well as breaking world records, I've used my memory to pass all my exams, give talks and demonstrations, remember all the people I meet, improve my sporting skills, win at games and quizzes – and I'm using it right now to pass on all my knowledge to you in this book!

I discovered the secrets of memory and now I'm going to explain how you too can benefit from the power of your mind. By the time you finish reading this book, you'll know how your memory works and how to use it to remember lists, facts and figures, names, dates, recipes, jokes.... You'll get better marks in school tests and exams, you'll be able to give talks and speeches from memory, you'll be more confident when meeting new people, you'll be more organised than ever before – in fact, you'll understand how to use your memory to do everything better.

You'll impress your family and friends but I bet you'll amaze yourself even more. Don't tell me that you've got a brain like a sieve. I'm going to prove to you that it can perform phenomenal mind-blowing facts.

It could change your life too!

Jonathan

Contents

What is memory?

Memory has fascinated people for thousands of years. Human beings have fantastic memories. Before they could write things down, they had to remember everything in their heads. They found out how to do new things and developed customs and rituals. They learned and remembered how to talk. Everything they knew – information and stories – was passed on by word of mouth.

Today, we have lots of memory aids to help us but we also have more information to remember. We can read books and write things down, but first we have to remember how to form the letters and words. We have to learn and remember how to use computers. So memory plays an even more vital part in our lives. But what is memory?

Amazing but true!

Since ancient times, people have built memorials such as statues. One of the most amazing memorials is Mount Rushmore in the USA. The faces of four Presidents, Washington, Jefferson, Roosevelt and Lincoln, have been carved directly into the rock of the mountain. George Washington's head is an incredible 20 metres high, and the whole thing took 14 years to complete. But it was worth it. Those four men will never be forgotten now!

A powerful force

Nobody knows for sure what memory is. The more closely scientists look at the brain, the less they feel certain about it. Memory is one of the most complicated, amazing and exciting things about the whole human body.

People have been trying to describe memory since ancient times. We know that it was a subject for debate as early as the sixth century BC. In those days, people thought memory was a very physical force – something to do with heat and cold, or dark and light, or the way the air was circulated in the body. Alter the arrangement of the air or change the physical conditions, they thought, and a memory could be lost forever.

The Ancient Greeks thought memory was like writing on a wax tablet. Somehow, words, facts, numbers and ideas were etched on to the brain but would then fade away with time, like the wax tablet gradually becoming smooth again.

Like a computer?

Other theories were that memory involved tiny parts of the brain organising themselves into precise arrangements, or that it was like a system of hydraulics, or clockwork....

Through the ages, many theories have come and gone but none of them has ever really explained what memory is.

Now that computers are so commonplace, human memory has often been compared with electronic memory. It would be handy if memory did work just like a computer. We'd be able to understand how information is taken in and filed away, and how best to get it out again. Unfortunately, scientists are discovering that computers and brains work very differently.

Amazing but true!

Sir Winston Churchill, one of Britain's greatest Prime Ministers, had an incredible memory. He's said to have memorised Milton's huge work, Paradise Lost, *in a week!*

What's the difference?

A computer either retrieves all the information – or it's broken. It doesn't have 'off days', it never gets tired or confused. It simply gives you back whatever you put in.

Your mind may be slow and inaccurate at times but there are occasions when it works faster than any computer and retrieves many more different types of information. Memories can be sparked off in a great variety of ways, with one thing jogging your mind about something else. In a split second, smells, sounds, names, dates, ideas and feelings all come rushing back.

Human memories are far less predictable than computers – but much more exciting.

Amazing but true!

The Cray supercomputer is one of the most powerful computers ever built. It weighs 7 tonnes and can carry out 400,000,000 calculations every second. Yet it would take a century to manage the amount of thinking your brain can do in one minute!

A hologram?

One interesting suggestion is that the brain works like a hologram. If you've ever seen a hologram, you'll know how amazing these pictures are. They're made using lasers, and because they combine pictures from different angles, they look three-dimensional and incredibly realistic. What's even more impressive, though, is what happens when you smash a hologram. If you break an ordinary picture, you end up with lots of bits of picture. But if you break a hologram, each little piece still contains the whole picture – just a little faded.

Perhaps your brain works like a hologram and each memory isn't just kept in one place, it's everywhere.

Amazing but true!

Seneca was a great writer and teacher in Ancient Rome. He had an incredible memory and would wake up his students by asking 200 of them to call out a line of poetry each. He would then read all the lines back from memory – forwards and backwards!

Where is the memory?

For a long time, most people believed that memory was more likely to work from the heart than the head! It was only about 500 years ago that everyone agreed that your mind was definitely between your ears!

If you've ever seen one of those china heads marked out into different sections, you might think that we know exactly where the memory is. The heads were designed to help people study 'phrenology', the art of reading character from the shape of the head. The phrenologists believed that the brain could be divided into different areas, like love, smell, problem-solving and memory. But – you've guessed it – it's not as simple as that. Some people are born with whole areas of their brain missing, or suffer from brain damage in accidents, and yet still manage to carry out a wide range of brain functions.

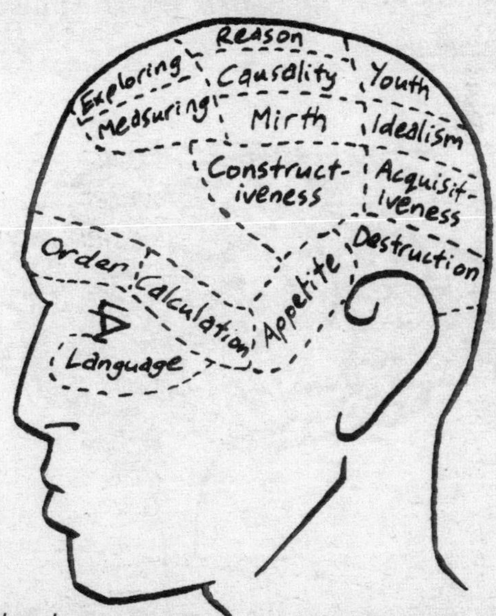

A phrenology head

Another time, another place

A scientist called Wilder Penfield tried stimulating different parts of people's brains (while they were still awake!) and found that touching specific areas made his patients remember very specific things. They would recall details like the smell and sound of a particular place and time. They remembered so clearly that they believed they were experiencing it all again. For a while, Penfield thought he had discovered where the brain stored different memories – but no such luck. It turned out that his patients could remember the same things even when that particular section of their brain was removed.

Penfield's research is still fascinating because it suggests that everything we ever experience is stored away somewhere in the brain, in perfect detail. But we still don't know where.

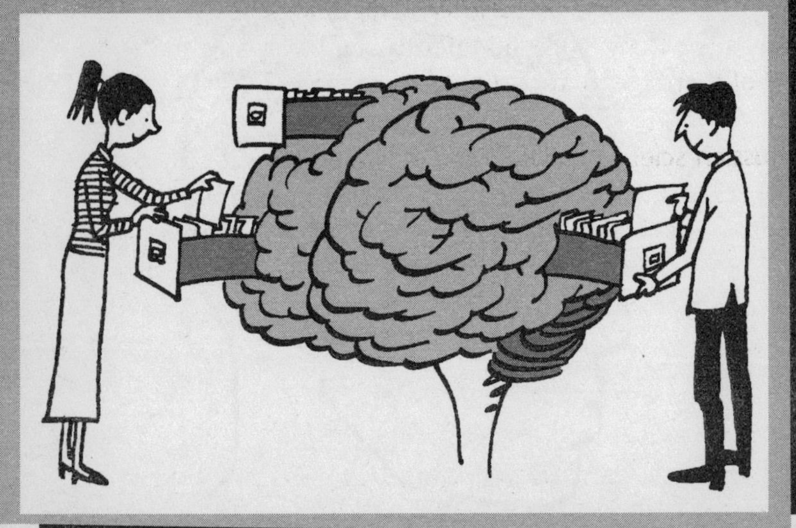

So what do we know about the brain?

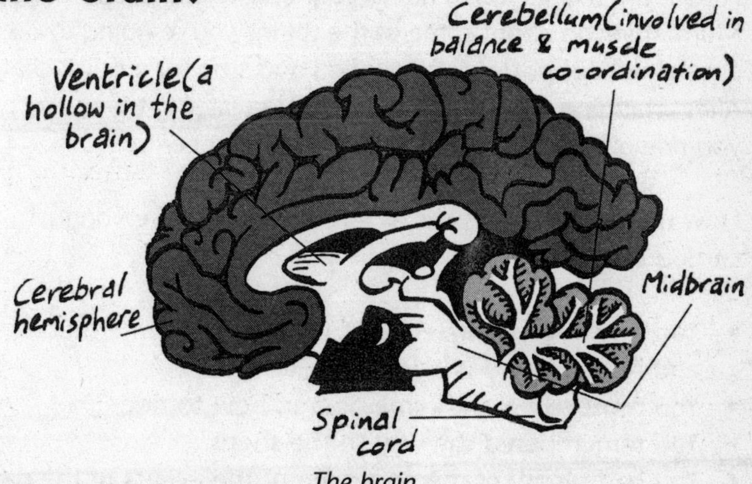

The brain

The brain is about the size of two clenched fists and it's amazingly light. We know that thinking and memory are handled in the enormous cerebral hemispheres, where about a billion cells called neurons form interconnected patterns. A neuron is less than one-hundredth of a millimetre across, so 250 of them could fit on the head of a pin.

A Russian scientist called Petr Anokhin once set out to calculate how many different connections a human brain could make. The number he came up with is extremely big. To write it down, you would need to write a 1 and then *ten and a half kilometres of noughts!*

Amazing facts about the brain

It is the only organ in the body that doesn't feel pain.
The average person knows between 20 and 100,000 words.
You have 10 billion brain cells but an ant has just 20.

Different kinds of memory

Picture the scene. You're riding your bike to the shops for your Mum, thinking about some of the things you're going to do at school. You spot your best friend and stop for a quick chat. After arranging to meet to go swimming later in the week, you ride off in the direction of the shopping centre.

How many different types of remembering have you just carried out?

- You saw a set of wheels held together by some metal and remembered it was your bike.
- You climbed on and remembered how to ride.
- You remembered the way to the shops.
- You had plenty of memories about the events of the day.
- You recognised your friend.
- When you chatted, you remembered what each word meant and could hold enough words in your mind to make sense of long sentences.
- You decided to remember something in the future – to go swimming.
- You set off again to see how much of your Mum's shopping you'd remember.

Storing in your brain

These are just some of the many different kinds of memory you use every single day. This is one of the reasons why the human memory is so complicated and so different from a computer's memory. It works in such a variety of ways.

Some things you would never forget – what a bike was, what your best friend looked like, how to talk, what words mean.

Other things must be stored differently in your brain because you could start to forget them in time. If you moved away and came back 50 years later, you might find it tricky to remember the way to the shops. Your Mum only told you what she needed a few minutes ago but will you remember it all? And what about remembering to go swimming? How often do arrangements like that slip your mind?

When you think about it, you certainly don't just have one memory!

Why should I improve my memory?

You may think you've got a good memory already. Answer the following questions to find out how useful a better memory would be to you.

- Would you like better marks in school tests?
- Could you improve at your favourite sports?
- Do you enjoy learning facts about movie or music stars?
- Would you like to be able to speak confidently in front of a group without reading out your speech?
- Would you be pleased if your homework took you less time?
- Have you ever forgotten something on a shopping list, missed someone's birthday or left something on a bus?

Throughout history, the most successful people have often been those with the best memories. In this book, you'll read about some of them and get ideas about what you could do with a trained mind.

Between your ears, there's an awful lot of brain power waiting to be used. Get ready to start flexing those memory muscles.

Test your memory

1 Which of the following Presidents of the United States is featured on the Mount Rushmore monument?

(a) Reagan (b) Truman
(c) Washington (d) Kennedy

2 The Ancient Greeks believed that memory was like which of these?

(a) a fountain (b) a wax tablet
(c) the planets (d) a musical instrument

3 Which Prime Minister memorised *Paradise Lost*?

(a) Churchill (b) Thatcher
(c) Eden (d) Macmillan

4 What are pictures using laser lights called?

(a) holographs (b) holophytes
(c) holograms (d) holotypes

5 How many brain cells do you have?

(a) a thousand (b) a million
(c) ten million (d) a billion

Answers: 1 (c) 2 (b) 3 (a) 4 (c) 5 (d)

What's your memory like now?

How good is your memory now? Here's a challenge for you. Look at the 26-digit number below. You have one minute to memorise it perfectly.

6 6 3 2 1 4 6 6 3 1 5 4 3 3 5 6 3 3 3 5 3 7 3 6 8 5

Time's up – so how did you do? Not too well?

Perhaps there's an easier way to do it. Here's how to improve your memory instantly. The secret to remembering this particular number is a nursery rhyme, *Humpty Dumpty*.

Humpty Dumpty sat on a wall,
Humpty Dumpty had a great fall,
All the king's horses and all the king's men
Couldn't put Humpty together again.

Each number stands for the number of letters in a word. The first word in the rhyme is 'Humpty' so the first number is **6**. 'Dumpty' has six letters too, then 'sat' has three, 'on' has two, and so on.

See how quickly you can write down all 26 numbers from memory.

It's easy!

In just a few minutes, you've improved your memory dramatically! You had no problem remembering the rhyme so you could remember the numbers too. All memory tricks are like this. You make it easier for yourself by changing information into a form you can deal with. You already have an excellent memory. You just have to learn the best way to use it.

I learnt the tricks of memory and became World Champion. Now I can remember 100 people's names in five minutes. I can memorise a pack of shuffled playing cards in less than a minute. I can remember a telephone number 2000 digits long.

Amazing but true!

On 24 June 1996, the American Dave Farrow memorised the order of 52 packs of playing cards all shuffled together – with just six mistakes!

In Harbin, China, a man called Gon Yang Ling memorised 15,000 numbers from the telephone directory.

So now you can see that your memory can be improved by learning some tricks. Here are some more tests to see how much you need to improve. You'll need a pen and some paper to jot down the answers, and the points you score.

Test 1: Objects

Give yourself a couple of minutes to read through this list of objects.

book coat key bottle iron kettle glass dog

watch table ring envelope pen comb knife

stone pin hat shoe phone

Now cover up the list. Here is another list. Can you spot the five new words in it?

watch dog phone lamp stone bracelet

bottle knife coat glass ball hat shoe comb

envelope torch chair table key ring

And what about the five words that are missing?

That's 10 answers altogether. When you think you've worked out as many as you can, look back at the first list to check how successful you were.

Give yourself a point for each correct answer and make a note of your score.

Test 2: Telephone numbers

Here are five imaginary telephone numbers. You have five minutes to memorise as many of them as you can.

cinema	**81403**
library	**22609**
swimming pool	**58716**
bookshop	**41931**
ice rink	**52687**

When the time's up, cover the numbers. Can you remember the phone number for the **bookshop**? What's the number for the **cinema**, the **ice rink**, the **swimming pool**, the **library**?

Give yourself four points for every number you remembered perfectly – so you could get 20 points here.

Test 3: Word list

This list of words has to be memorised in order. You have two minutes.

1 mountain 2 whale 3 fire 4 gate 5 song
6 taste 7 new 8 steaming 9 hole 10 long

Now cover up the list and try to write it out from memory.

Give yourself two points for each word you remembered and an extra two points for each one you remembered in the right order. If you remembered the whole list in order, that's 20 points.

Memory marvel

In recent times in New Zealand, the Maori chief Kaumatana could recite the entire history of his tribe. The names and stories went back through 45 generations and covered more than 1000 years. It took chief Kaumatana more than three days of non-stop remembering to tell the whole amazing tale.

Test 4: Questionnaire

Can you remember:

anything before you were four years old?	(Yes/No)
anything before you were three?	(Yes/No)
anything before you were two?	(Yes/No)
your first day at school?	(Yes/No)
which months have 31 days?	(Yes/No)
the lyrics of your favourite song?	(Yes/No)
routes around your local area?	(Yes/No)
all your teachers' names?	(Yes/No)
a recipe?	(Yes/No)
your three best friends' birthdays?	(Yes/No)
the story of the last book you read?	(Yes/No)
five jokes?	(Yes/No)
your timetable at school?	(Yes/No)
your postcode?	(Yes/No)
where your bag is at this moment?	(Yes/No)

Give yourself two points for every 'Yes'.

Test 5: Names and faces

Spend two minutes looking at the 10 people shown below.

Cover up all the faces. How many of them can you remember? Write down any names you can recall, in the order that their owners appear here.

Give yourself one point for each first name and one for each surname you get right. The maximum here is 20 points.

How did you do?

That's the end of the memory test. Don't worry if you haven't done brilliantly. The whole point of this book is to boost your memory power, and you're going to be shown tricks to improve every area of your memory. To help you chart your progress, though, it's important to know where you're starting from.

To come up with your Starting Memory Level, simply add up your scores in each of the five memory tests.
The maximum score is 100.

This is how you did.

Less than 10:	**Poor**
11 - 30:	**Not bad**
31 - 50:	**Average**
51 - 70:	**Good**
71 - 90	**Excellent**
More than 90:	**Exceptional**

Memory marvel

In 1894, Napoleon Bird, a barber from Stockport in England, played the piano from memory for 44 hours without repeating a single composition.

Training tip

Doing several things at once may be a good way to train your memory. Your mind can cope with several different tasks simultaneously and, with practice, you can keep track of them all with ease. In fact, you may find your mind works better. I wrote most of this book whilst walking, cooking – and sometimes juggling!

Heard of Julius Caesar? This great Roman emperor had a phenomenal memory and taught himself to write more than one letter at once. He would dictate his thoughts to scribes, who wrote down whatever he said. The Roman historian Pliny reported that Caesar could dictate as many as seven letters at the same time.

Amazing but true!

In one year, passengers on trains in Japan forgot

half a million umbrellas,
400,000 articles of clothing,
72 pairs of false teeth,
seven boxes of human ashes.

The watch test

Here's one last experiment for you to try. Cover up your wristwatch without looking at it. How many details about your watch can you remember?

- What shape is it?
- What colour is it?
- Does it have hands and, if so, what do they look like?
- Is there a digital display? Where is it exactly?
- How is the strap designed?
- What other details set your watch apart?

When you've remembered as much as you can, uncover your watch and find out how well you did.

People who try the watch test are often amazed at how badly their memory performs. If you did OK, think of some other designs that you see many times a day – coins, bank logos, shopfronts. Can you remember them all?

Memory joggers

The watch test shows that just *seeing* something lots of times doesn't guarantee that you're going to remember it. If you're learning information – revising for a test, for example – it's no good just reading it through again and again. That kind of 'parrot fashion' learning is just boring, takes a long time – and it doesn't always work.

What about some of the popular 'memory joggers'? How many of these have you tried?

- Knotting a handkerchief.
- Leaving something in an unusual place.
- Writing on your hand.
- Making notes on scraps of paper.
- Asking someone else to remind you.

Tricks like these might work but how do you know you're going to remember what the knot in your handkerchief is for, or that you won't lose the bit of paper you've written something down on?

If you want to learn something properly, and have fun at the same time, you need to do things a different way. You need to know the 12 SRIs – the Secret Rules about Information.

Test your memory

How good is your general knowledge? You might be surprised at just how many facts you can recall. Test out your memory for everyday information with this fun quiz.

1 What is the capital of Australia?

(a) Canberra (b) Sydney
(c) Melbourne

2 Which of these wasn't one of the Seven Dwarfs?

(a) Sleepy (b) Sneezy
(c) Nosy

3 How many days are there in March?

(a) 29 (b) 30
(c) 31

4 Who wrote *Treasure Island*?

(a) Alexander Dumas (b) Robert Louis Stevenson
(c) Daniel Defoe

5 Which soccer team plays at Old Trafford?

(a) Manchester United (b) Liverpool
(c) Arsenal

6 What colour was the boat used by the owl and the pussycat?

(a) sea blue (b) pea green
(c) jet black

7 What are Drury Lane, The Palladium and Her Majesty's?

(a) theatres (b) hospitals
(c) law courts

8 What is Spiderman's real name?

(a) Patrick Painter (b) Paul Partner
(c) Peter Parker

9 How many items make up a baker's dozen?

(a) 12 (b) 13
(c) 14

10 Fill in the missing word: 'A stitch in time saves ......'

(a) nine (b) wine
(c) pine

Answers: 1 (a) 2 (c) 3 (c) 4 (b) 5 (a) 6 (b)
7 (a) 8 (c) 9 (b) 10 (a)

The Secret Rules about Information

To discover the secret rules, you need to do what I did when I wanted to find a way to memorise a pack of playing cards – ask a question:

'Why are some things more memorable than others?'

You'll begin to get some of the answers when you try the following experiment.

Get a friend to read these 25 words out loud to you. Then, straight away, write down as many of them as you can from memory.

box cat fence sycamore pencil bag horse-chestnut key ring glass fish chair pipe Tyrannosaurus Rex book house milk lightning oak barbecue fly van clock soap wall

Memory marvel

The people of the Senoi tribe, deep in the jungle of the Malay peninsular, have a strong tradition of remembering. In particular, they've taught themselves to remember their dreams. They talk about them with their families and friends each morning to find out if they hold any important messages for the future.

How did you do?

Most people are able to remember between seven and 10 words from the list, so if you scored more than 10, congratulations!

The reason for doing this experiment isn't really to find out how many words you remember, though. It's to look at *why* you remember them.

The words most often remembered are:

box cat fence sycamore horse-chestnut oak key ring Tyrannosaurus Rex barbecue lightning clock soap wall

Look back at the words you remembered. How many of them make it to this list?

Why do we remember these?

box, cat, fence: People tend to remember these first three words because their minds were fresh and alert when the test started, they were interested in the sorts of words they were going to hear, and they were trying hard to make their memories work.

sycamore, horse-chestnut, oak: Most people spot that there are three linked words in the list – the three trees – and remember them as a group.

key, ring: These two words fit together – key-ring – and often stick in people's minds as one 'chunk' of memory.

Tyrannosaurus Rex: I bet you remembered the king of the dinosaurs! An unusual word like this makes you take notice so it's much easier to remember than the other, more everyday words.

Amazing but true!

The long, exciting play Hamlet by William Shakespeare is memorable to audiences – but the actor playing the title role has to have an incredible memory. He has to remember 1539 lines!

lightning: This word is very visual and the sort of image that sticks in the memory. Everyone can picture a dramatic flash of lightning.

barbecue: This word makes your senses work, and the senses are very important to the whole memory process. Can you imagine the smell of hot food cooking on the barbecue? How do the juicy hamburgers and sizzling sausages taste?

clock, soap, wall: These words are easy to remember simply because they're at the very end of the list. You have very little time to forget them and there are no new words afterwards to confuse you.

Amazing but true!

Although elephants are supposed to have the best memories in the animal world, that title should perhaps go to the dolphin. Researchers at the Severstow Insitute in Moscow have discovered that a dolphin can listen to half an hour of 'clicks' from another dolphin and then repeat them, keeping exactly the same length and pitch.

The forgettable words

So much for the words people remember. What about the ones they forget?

The most forgettable words on this list seem to be:

pencil bag glass fish chair pipe book house milk

What do these words have in common? They're all simple, dull, everyday words and they're all from the middle section of the list. They don't make you take notice, they don't excite your senses, they're not connected together, and they don't spark off any interesting or unusual pictures in your mind.

So, what are the 12 Secret Rules about Information?

The first seven rules

You are more likely to **remember** something if it's

- at the start.
- at the end.
- connected to other things in a group.
- connected to something else as a single chunk.
- unusual.
- visual.
- stimulating to the senses.

The next five rules

You are more likely to **forget** something if it's

- in the middle.
- not connected to anything else.
- boring.
- not visual.
- not stimulating to the senses.

Putting the rules to good use

Once you know the 12 Secret Rules about Information, it's easy to guess which things are going to be memorable, and which forgettable. Try separating the following types of information into two lists – 'memorable' and 'forgettable' – then look at the next page to check your success.

- A telephone number.
- What you did on your last birthday.
- Famous paintings.
- A shopping list.
- Cartoon characters.
- Postcodes.
- A thrilling film.
- Jobs you have to do.
- The words of your current favourite song.

Memory marvel

In his old age, South African politician Jan Christian Smuts memorised 5000 books.

Answers to the 'memorable' and 'forgettable' test

Memorable

What you did on your last birthday (an unusual, exciting day).

Famous paintings (visual).

Cartoon characters (visual, funny, exciting).

A thrilling film (exciting, unusual, connected scenes).

The words of your current favourite song (words connected into sentences, notes connected into catchy tunes).

Forgettable

A telephone number (boring, unconnected digits).

A shopping list (dull, unconnected items).

Postcodes (boring, unconnected numbers and letters).

Jobs you have to do (dull information, not visual, not stimulating to the senses).

So it's clear that some types of information are a great deal easier to remember than others.

Memory rhymes

For centuries, people have been writing poems to remind them of important information – and to practise their memory skills.

How many of these memory rhymes have you used?

Thirty days hath September,
April, June and November.
All the rest have thirty-one
Excepting February alone,
And that has twenty-eight days clear
And twenty-nine in each leap year.

Columbus sailed the ocean blue
In fourteen hundred and ninety-two.

The Spanish Armada met its fate
In fifteen hundred and eighty-eight.

In sixteen hundred and sixty-six
London burnt like rotten sticks.

Spring is showery, flowery, bowery,
Summer: hoppy, croppy, poppy,
Autumn: slippy, drippy, nippy.
Winter: breezy, sneezy, freezy.

A was an Apple pie,
B Bit it,
C Cut it,
D Dealt it,
E Eats it,
F Fought for it,
G Got it,
H Had it,
I Inspected it,
J Joined for it,
K Kept it,
L Longed for it,
M Mourned for it,
N Nodded at it,
O Opened it,
P Peeped in it,
Q Quartered it,
R Ran for it,
S Stole it,
T Took it,
U Upset it,
V Viewed it, W Wanted it,
XYZ all wished for a piece in hand!

When the wind is in the East
'Tis neither good for man nor beast.
When the wind is in the North
The skilful fisher goes not forth.
When the wind is in the South
It blows the bait in the fish's mouth.
When the wind is in the West
Then it is at its very best.

Test your memory

1 Who wrote the play *Hamlet*?

(a) Ben Jonson (b) William Shakespeare
(c) John Webster (d) John Gay

2 Which tribe of people remember their dreams?

(a) Onise (b) Oseni
(c) Isone (d) Senoi

3 Which animal may have a better memory than an elephant?

(a) a dolphin (b) an ant
(c) a cow (d) a camel

4 What nationality was Jan Smuts?

(a) American (b) South African
(c) Spanish (d) English

5 Which dinosaur featured on the word list?

(a) Tyrannosaurus Rex (b) Velociraptor
(c) Triceratops (d) Iguanodon

Answers: 1 (b) 2 (d) 3 (a) 4 (b) 5 (a)

4 Make the information easier to remember

The trick to developing a super-power memory is to *change* the difficult information to make it more memorable.

Read that sentence again because it's the key to remembering.

That's the best-kept secret of all. You don't have to struggle with information in the form in which it's given to you. If it's hard to remember, you can play around with it in your mind until it's as easy to remember as a thrilling film or the words of your favourite song.

You're going to learn some amazing strategies for making information memorable, but there are two things to consider first – *why* you want to remember something and whether you can use your surroundings to help you.

Why do I want to remember?

What were you doing three months ago today? You probably don't know. But what if I said I'd give you a million pounds if you could tell me? I bet you'd rack your brains and find some way of remembering!

What's in it for me?

Having a reason to do something is always important but it's absolutely crucial for remembering. Trying to remember the chores you have to do or the times of school lessons you don't enjoy is difficult because you don't feel very motivated. You're at a disadvantage before you start.

Always think of the reason why you're trying to remember something. What are you going to get out of it? Perhaps it's to get better marks in a test, achieve a higher grade in a dance competition, win a sports quiz – or just amaze your friends by remembering their birthdays.

There's always a good reason so, rather than moaning about it and hating every second, do everything you can to boost your motivation. You could give yourself treats for doing a certain amount of revision, or for remembering enough words in a spelling test or songs in a pop quiz. Always make sure you have a reason for wanting to learn and remember.

How's that for motivation?

The highest prize ever for a mental challenge was five million dollars, which was shared by the chess players Bobby Fischer and Boris Spassky for their match in 1992. Would that be enough to motivate you to strain your muscles in a game of chess?

Be confident you can do it

Along with motivation, confidence is the other key feeling when you're trying to remember things. Most people say they have a 'terrible memory' and tell themselves and anyone who'll listen that they always forget everything. It's no wonder that they do!

Top athletes need to be super-confident and they practise focusing on success. If they thought they were going to lose, they most probably would.

The weight-lifting test

Here's an excellent example of the importance of confidence – whatever you're doing.

For a long time 500 lb* was seen as the limit in weight-lifting. Everyone thought it was impossible to beat.

A Russian weight-lifter called Vasily Alexeyev had won the gold medal in the 1976 Olympics and was determined to lift more than 500 lb – but it was indeed proving impossible. He could lift almost 500 lb but every time he tried 500 lb exactly, no matter how hard he strained, the bar was just too heavy.

Vasily's lack of confidence was holding him back. He had come to believe that 500 lb was too heavy for anyone to lift and so his mind was stopping his body from working properly.

* A pound (lb) is an Imperial unit of weight. 1 lb is equal to 2.2 kg.

Luckily for Vasily, he had some very cunning trainers. They realised that it was his lack of confidence that was the problem, so one day at training, they told him that he was going to try to lift 499.9 lb. He was pretty confident of managing that – it was just less than the dreaded 500 lb. Sure enough, he was able to lift it successfully.

But then the trainers weighed the bar in front of Vasily and showed him that he'd actually lifted 501.5 lb – they'd secretly added extra weights!

The 500-lb milestone had been passed and it was no longer a source of fear for Vasily – or for any other world-standard weight-lifter. All around the world, people starting lifting greater and greater weights.

At the Olympics a few years later, Vasily Alexeyev, who'd had so much trouble with 500 lb, managed to lift 564 lb!

Being confident is a vital part of the memory process. Believe in yourself and in the memory tricks you're learning, and you will remember more.

Be in the right place

If you had to revise for an exam, prepare for an assessment or learn lines for a play, where would you go? Where would you learn best?

It makes sense to think about the sort of conditions you need to make your mind work effectively. You need to get them right to create your own Memory Zone.

Ask yourself these questions:

Memory Zone checklist

- Do you like to do things indoors or outside?
- Do you prefer to sit down or walk about?
- Do you work best on your own or with a friend?
- Do you need music in the background or do you prefer silence?

Perfect silence

The writer Marcel Proust lined his workroom with cork to keep out any noise and create his perfect thinking environment.

Now find the place that suits you best

Too many people waste time struggling to learn in places that simply don't suit them. Always spend time preparing your Memory Zone and it'll save you time, make your learning more effective – and make memory seem much less like hard work.

If you use the same place regularly for working or learning, you'll get used to working there. Your brain will get an automatic boost just by being in the familiar place.

Here's what they did

English poet Samuel Johnson needed to hear the purring of his cat, while the German playwright Friedrich Schiller found that the smell of rotting apples helped him to think.

For Sherlock Holmes, of course, the best place to think and remember was the study of 221B Baker Street in London, where he could smoke his pipe – and play the violin as loudly as he liked.

How accurate is your memory?

What's your earliest memory? When asked that question, many people feel very confident about a particular place or event from early in their lives. Think about your earliest memory now: what images, sounds, smells and feelings come to mind?

But perhaps your memory is playing tricks on you. Are you sure that these memories are real? Do you really remember them?

The basic memories might be true but are the details correct? It's fun to do some detective work. Find photographs, films or videos and ask friends and members of your family if they can confirm or deny the accuracy of your memories. Don't worry if some things aren't true after all, because research suggests that everyone's mind works like this. It's a bit like the game of Chinese Whispers: every time we remember something from the past, we change it slightly and the changes are what we remember next time around. The details you remember may eventually be very different from what really happened, even if you feel convinced that your earliest memories are 100 per cent accurate.

Test your memory

1 Name Boris Spassky's opponent.

(a) Barry Butcher (b) Benny Painter
(c) Billy Fitter (d) Bobby Fischer

2 What is Vasily Alexeyev's sport?

(a) weight-lifting (b) diving
(c) football (d) shot putting

3 What was Samuel Johnson's favourite pet?

(a) a fish (b) a cat
(c) a dog (d) a budgie

4 What did Proust use to keep his workroom quiet?

(a) cotton wool (b) paper
(c) cork (d) egg boxes

5 What was the name of the street where Sherlock Holmes lived?

(a) Baker Street (b) Barker Street
(c) Biker Street (d) Boxer Street

Answers: 1 (d) 2 (a) 3 (b) 4 (c) 5 (a)

5 Making memory links

You're feeling motivated and confident, you've found a good place to sit and you know what it is that makes information memorable. Now, how do you go about learning it and performing amazing feats of memory? There's one answer to this – imagination.

Great imaginations

The Emperor Napoleon once said, 'Imagination rules the world'. Napoleon had a huge store of technical information, and he used his imagination to learn it and practise it before going into battle.

Albert Einstein said that imagination was more important than knowledge. To help him work out his famous theory of relativity, he pictured himself sitting on a beam of light, holding a clock!

Imagination lets you explore information in order to understand it – and also to change it to make it more interesting, exciting, fun and *memorable.*

Remember the 26 numbers you memorised earlier, with a little help from Humpty Dumpty? That was an example of how boring, forgettable information can be made memorable in your mind if you play around with it a little.

Anything can be made to fit in with the way your mind works best. Remember the 12 Secret Rules about Information? Here are the key stages which will help you to make what you have to learn suit those rules.

Organising

This means looking at the way something is organised already and thinking about how you can rearrange it to make it easier to handle.

Let's say you were learning a list of words for a test at school. You would need to look at how the information was organised. You will find it easier to remember the first and last parts of the list, so it is important to spend a little more time learning the middle sections.

When it comes to organising the information yourself, there are several tricks you can try.

Changing the order

Which is easier to remember:
8301254679 or **0123456789**?

Obviously it's the second list of numbers because they're organised in a logical way. But it's basically the same information, re-organised to make it easier to handle.

Grouping

Which would you find easier to remember:
aglw or **aeroplane goat lemonade Wednesday**?

My guess is that there's not much difference between the two, but the second group holds a lot more information – 30 letters compared with just four. Your memory finds it no harder to remember four groups of letters than four single letters, so it makes sense to learn groups of information wherever possible.

Connecting

When you get to the end of a book or film, you can remember what happened because of the connections. One bit of the story leads on to another, one scene takes you on to the next, and you can recall a large amount of information.

The same happens in songs. It's difficult to remember a song if you have to start in the middle – but start at the beginning and each line will jog your memory and lead you on to the next.

You can connect other types of information in the same kind of way, but you need to use your imagination to make the connections memorable. For example, imagine you have to learn this shopping list:

potatoes chocolate soap milk bread tuna bin-bags spaghetti

The items on the list aren't connected in any way – but they can be if you use your imagination. You can make up a weird story to link them all together. Prepare to let your imagination go wild.

Make up a story

Perhaps your story could begin with you peeling a large potato. To your surprise, as you peel off the skin, you find that the inside is made of solid chocolate. You can't resist having a bite – but it's disgusting! The chocolate tastes of soap! Soap bubbles start coming out of your mouth. One of the bubbles looks different from the rest and when it bursts, you realise why – it's full of milk! The milk sloshes all over the floor. Soon it's so deep that you have to climb on to a raft made from pieces of bread. There are huge tuna fish swimming around your raft and you catch one in a bin-bag. The fish writhes around inside, so you tie up the bin-bag with a long, thin piece of spaghetti.

Read the story through once more, then close your eyes. Go back through the chain of events in your mind and call out the eight items as you come to them.

It all started when you were peeling a potato which turned out to be made from solid....

Picturing

Being able to picture something in your mind's eye is a key step towards remembering it. We all have an incredible memory for pictures.

Researchers in America once carried out an experiment to see just how many different pictures people could recall at once. They showed some volunteers 2560 slides, each one carrying the image of an object, person or landmark. The slides were flashed on to a screen for a few seconds at a time. Later, they showed the same people 2560 pairs of slides. In each pair was one of the pictures shown earlier. Would they remember which one they'd already seen, A or B?

When all the testing was over, they checked the group's scores – and the results were amazing! Everyone tested had been able to recall almost every one of the 2560 slides seen earlier. The general success rate was better than 90 per cent.

The mind's capacity for remembering pictures is practically limitless. We find it much easier to remember images than words, which is why people often recognise a face but can't put a name to it. The more colourful and detailed the picture is, the better – so it makes sense to use strong mental images when you're trying to make your memory work.

'Seeing' information

Here are a couple of exercises to help you practise 'seeing' information vividly in your mind's eye. Prepare to give your imagination muscles a good stretch!

Look at the 10 words printed below. Read each one in turn and spend about half a minute *picturing* it in your mind. Try to bring in as many colours as possible and to be as detailed as you can. Once you've fixed the image in your mind, see if you can imagine viewing it from different angles.

car apple mountain book kite coat piano elephant door train

The more you use it, the more powerful your imagination will become. As well as picturing objects in your mind, you'll be able to imagine things happening to them. Just like the shopping list earlier, you'll be able to bring *any* list to life in your mind and picture a vivid, memorable story.

Connecting what you see

Now to the next stage – connecting the pictures you have visualised. Here is a list of eight Christmas presents. It would be very useful to be able to commit a list like this to memory. You wouldn't have to write it down, fumble with a scrap of paper in busy shops, or come back home without all the right gifts.

You have five minutes to memorise the list.

chocolates tie watch umbrella board-game radio soap pen

STEP 1: Picture each item, giving it detail and colour.

STEP 2: Think up a story that connects all eight items together. You need to link the chocolates with the tie, the tie with the watch, the watch with the umbrella, and so on. There are some ideas to help you on the next page.

Top tip

Whenever you learn a country's capital city, try to fix the city and the country names in your mind as one group. Get used to thinking of 'Parisfrance' (Paris, the capital of France), 'Canberraaustralia' (Canberra, the capital of Australia), Bogotacolombia (Bogota, the capital of Colombia) and so on. By doing this, you can trick your mind into learning two bits of information for the price of one!

A story idea

Here's an idea for a story to connect the presents on the Christmas list.

You might imagine melting the **chocolates** and pressing them flat to turn them into a **tie**. Instead of putting the tie round your neck, though, you might imagine knotting it around your **watch**. The watch might have a huge **umbrella** fixed to it, to keep off the rain. You could decide to gather some friends together to sit on top of the umbrella and play a **board-game**. Perhaps one of your friends annoys you by playing his **radio** full blast while you're trying to concentrate on the game. You could cover the radio with a thick layer of **soap** to sabotage it. Maybe your friend tries to scrape the soap off with a **pen**.

If those were your links, you'd easily be able to remember squashing chocolates into the shape of a tie, wrapping it around your watch with the umbrella attached, sitting on the umbrella to play the board-game, and so on. Each part of the story jogs your memory and takes you to the next part.

Spend a few minutes either imagining the story above or thinking up your own, then cover up the list and see if you can remember all eight Christmas presents.

Ideas for remembering countries

You might need to learn a list of countries for a test at school. How would you do it? Look at this list.

France Turkey America Wales China Scotland Holland Italy

You could easily think of a memorable image to represent each country. It might be something that country is famous for making, a landmark, or even something that sounds or looks like the country's name. Then you connect the images.

Here are some ideas:

France	the Eiffel Tower
Turkey	a gobbling turkey
America	a cowboy's lasso
Wales	whales
China	a pile of china plates
Scotland	a kilt
Holland	a pair of clogs
Italy	the Leaning Tower of Pisa

Now for the connecting story

You might imagine that every level of the Eiffel Tower is full of turkeys. One of them is using a lasso to catch whales swimming around below. The whales try to escape and they swim straight into a tall pile of china plates, bringing them crashing to the ground. You use an old kilt to wrap up the bits of broken china before tipping them all into a huge pair of clogs that you are using as a dustbin. Perhaps one of the clogs is now so full that it leans over like the Leaning Tower of Pisa!

Read the story through a couple of times and make sure you use your imagination to the full. Picture it all in your mind's eye as vividly as you can.

Now can you cover up the list and write out the eight countries from memory? Simply go back through the strange story in your mind, pick out the key images and use each one to remind you of a country.

Remember, it all started when you noticed that the Eiffel Tower was full of turkeys....

The words in the middle

Whenever you learn a list like the eight countries, make sure you spend a little extra time on the words in the middle. As you saw earlier, they're always harder to remember than the ones at the start or the end. It's a useful way to organise your time while you're also organising the information by connecting images into a story.

Memory marvel

An American military man, General George Marshall, demonstrated his amazing memory regularly at press conferences. He had to talk to the media on many different topics and developed a particular strategy for dealing with questions. He told people to ask him whatever they wanted, while he was talking. He never answered them there and then, but would wait until he had finished his main speech. Often, the people who'd asked the questions would now have their answers. If not, he was able to talk to each of them in turn, explaining whatever they wanted to know. He never made notes. He simply used the sort of memory tricks you have been learning in this book. A powerful memory meant that he never lost his train of thought, never wasted people's time and impressed everyone with his organisation and precision.

So, to recap, you organise and you picture. A good way to practise both these key memory skills is to play a game.

Kim's Game

Gather together between 10 and 15 items on a tray or table. Give yourself a few minutes to memorise the collection by doing exactly what you did to learn the shopping lists or the eight countries. After looking at each object, visualise it in your mind's eye. Connect the first object to the second, the second to the third and so on, to create a vivid memory story.

As soon as you're confident that you know all the items, get a friend to remove one of them secretly. How quickly can you say which one's missing? Simply go back through the memory story in your mind until you come to the object that's no longer there.

Challenge other friends to a game. Who'll call out the correct object first? Once you've had fun amazing everyone with your super-power memory, you could explain some of the tricks to your friends, then see who can memorise the most objects in the fastest time.

Test your memory

1 Who said 'Imagination rules the world'?

(a) Cleopatra (b) Napoleon
(c) Nero (d) Nelson

2 Who imagined riding on a beam of light?

(a) Einstein (b) Edison
(c) Eiffel (d) Eliot

3 What nationality was George Marshall?

(a) German (b) Australian
(c) French (d) American

4 What was his rank?

(a) corporal (b) major
(c) lieutenant (d) general

5 In the famous picture experiment, what form were the images shown in?

(a) engravings (b) paintings
(c) slides (d) cartoons

Answers: 1 (b) 2 (a) 3 (d) 4 (d) 5 (c)

Make things larger than life

You saw earlier how important it is for information to be unusual if you're going to stand a chance of remembering it. Unfortunately, a lot of the information you're presented with is pretty dull and boring – so you have to use your imagination to make it more interesting.

Exaggerating

Exaggerating something will make it stand out. In your mind's eye, you can do anything you want to it. You could make your pictures huge or tiny, brightly coloured, loud, moving, talking. The funnier the stories, the more you'll remember them, and it's often possible to use exaggeration to great comic effect.

Think of some of the things that happen in cartoons. Objects explode, change suddenly, do and say silly things – and all the images are colourful and memorable.

Here's an exercise to help you practise exaggerating.

Read these 10 words and then spend a few moments picturing them in your imagination and exaggerating them. How can you make these simple words unusual, exciting and funny?

cake key cow ball flower bed banana camera lamp ice-cream

Connections again

When you've got the hang of exaggerating, try memorising the list of 10 words below. Be confident – you know enough memory tricks by now to learn information like this easily. Simply follow the key steps.

STEP 1: Picture each word in turn.
STEP 2: Exaggerate your picture.
STEP 3: Connect it to the next word, then connect that word to the next and so on.
STEP 4: Use exaggeration again to make all the connections as powerful as you can.

Here's the list:

castle sheep fire tea fly newspaper car hole torch crown

You've got five minutes to turn this list of words into a memory story. When the time's up, cover up the words and see how many of them you can remember, in order.

Memory marvel

The world-renowned conductor Arturo Toscanini had an incredible memory for music. On one occasion, a worried bassoon player came running up to him before a long concert to say that one of the keys on his bassoon had broken. It was too late to get it fixed and no suitable replacement could be found.

Toscanini ran through all the music for the performance in his mind. He was able to remember every note due to be played by every single instrument in the orchestra and so could reassure the man that he didn't need to worry about a broken key that night.

On another occasion, when Toscanini was performing with the NBC Orchestra in New York, he decided that he wanted them to play a piece by a composer called Joachim Raff. The piece wasn't very well known and the music couldn't be found anywhere in the city, so Toscanini wrote down the entire piece from memory. Later, when the original music was found, it showed that in all his thousands of notes and markings, Toscanini had made just one small mistake.

Getting involved

You remember birthdays, Christmas mornings and holidays because you were involved in what was going on and the feelings you had were strong ones – excitement, happiness, delight. Powerful feelings are a crucial part of the memory process and you can use feelings, emotions and senses to make learning easier, faster and more fun.

Here's another list of 10 words. This time, as you picture each item on the list, try to bring in as many senses as possible. What does this thing smell like, sound like, feel like – even taste like?

ice-lolly horse lawnmower bonfire cooker drill firework piano sandwich kettle

Using your senses

How powerfully can you imagine senses and feelings?

Imagine you're holding a bright yellow lemon. You use a knife to cut it into two halves, and then you lick one of the open sides. As you think about it now, is your mouth watering?

Imagine you're standing in front of a blackboard. You scratch a rusty nail from the top to the bottom. Can you feel a shiver as you imagine the noise?

With a little practice, it's possible to imagine touching, smelling, tasting and hearing as vividly as things you can see.

Amazing but true!

In Ancient Greece, when a boundary line was being drawn up between two pieces of land, a young child was taken to the line and spanked! The idea was that the child would never forget the bad experience he had there and so would always remember the exact position of the boundary line.

Taking control

In your imagination you can take control of the information you have to learn. Instead of just reading words on a page, you can imagine playing around with the material, making it your own, doing things to it that you'll remember.

In the next exercise, you're going to be more violent than you've ever been before! You have to imagine destroying each object on the following list in the most devastating way. You might imagine pulling all the springs out of the clock and twisting the hands, pouring water into the computer, or dropping the goldfish bowl from the top floor of a tall building. Imagine what it feels like to ruin

a clock a computer a goldfish bowl a mirror a table
a tennis racket a shoe a bed a CD a pair of sunglasses

Now see how this helped

When you've had fun destroying those objects, see how well it's improved your memory. Cover up the list, then read through the second list below. There are three new items here, but can you spot which they are? Which of these items *didn't* you destroy?

a mirror   a computer   a cassette   a clock   a table
a toaster   a tennis racket   a bed   a mug   a shoe

When you think you've picked out the three new items, look back to the original list to check your success.

Top tip

The Renaissance artist Leonardo da Vinci believed that most people never take control of the information they're given. He said that they never really observe what things look like or feel like, and never take it in properly. He wrote that the average human 'looks without seeing, listens without hearing, touches without feeling, eats without tasting'. Take Leonardo's advice – always be observant and alive to your senses, and you'll be more likely to remember the information you're given.

Memory checklist

Here's a quick re-cap of the key points so far.

When you have to learn something, you need to

be motivated.

be confident.

organise the information, splitting it into groups or connecting it into a story.

picture it vividly.

exaggerate it.

get involved with it in your imagination.

Every time you create a memory story to learn a set of information, make sure you involve yourself as much as you can. Bring in senses and feelings and take control of the material you're given.

To practise all the memory techniques you've learned so far, how about another game?

Granny Went to Market

Here's how this fun and challenging game works. You need to play it with a group of people – between three and seven is ideal. The first person says, 'My granny went to market and she bought . . .' and then chooses something she might have picked up. So it could be, 'My granny went to market and she bought a puppy'.

The next person says, 'My granny went to market and she bought a puppy and . . .' and adds something else – let's say, a bottle of milk.

The third person then has to remember what's come so far before adding another item to the list. 'My granny went to market and she bought a puppy, a bottle of milk and a saxophone.'

The game continues with more and more items being added until someone makes a mistake and goes out. Everyone keeps playing until there's only one person left – the winner and the proud owner of the best memory in the group!

How to win the game every time!

The trick to this game is to treat the list of items Granny buys like any other list of words. Simply follow the steps in the Memory Checklist on page 72. Picture each item vividly, exaggerate it in some way, then connect it to the next item in a memorable story. Make it strange and funny, involve your senses and feelings.

Perhaps the puppy starts drinking the milk noisily before pouring the last few drops into the end of the priceless saxophone Granny has bought for you.

Trust in the memory tricks and there's no reason why you can't win the game every time. When that gets a bit boring, why not explain the winning techniques to your friends? Then you could compete with them to see who can get the record score. Would you be able to recall 20 words, 30 words? Using these tricks, I once memorised a list of 1000 words!

Did you know?

Memory techniques are known as ***mnemonics****. The word comes from Mnemosyne, the Goddess of Memory from the ancient world.*

Test your memory

1 Who was Toscanini?

(a) a conductor
(b) a painter
(c) a writer
(d) a singer

2 Who did Toscanini prove his memory skills to?

(a) a violinist
(b) a bassoonist
(c) a drummer
(d) a trumpeter

3 Boundaries were remembered by spanking children in which ancient civilisation?

(a) Egypt
(b) Rome
(c) Greece
(d) India

4 Who said most people 'look without seeing'?

(a) Winston Churchill
(b) Leonardo da Vinci
(c) Mozart
(d) Houdini

5 What are memory techniques called?

(a) mnemonics
(b) mechanics
(c) mesomorphs
(d) menorahs

Answers: 1 (a) 2 (b) 3 (c) 4 (b) 5 (a)

7 Memory frameworks

As well as connecting images together to form stories, you can use your imagination to fix them into frameworks. Your framework can be buildings you know well, or walks you enjoy taking.

The system goes back as far as the ancient world. Greek legend has it that a famous poet, teacher and memory expert called Simonides was a guest at a huge feast held by a millionaire called Scopas. Disaster struck when the roof of the banqueting hall caved in, crushing the people below. Simonides was the only survivor and it was up to him to identify the hundreds of bodies.

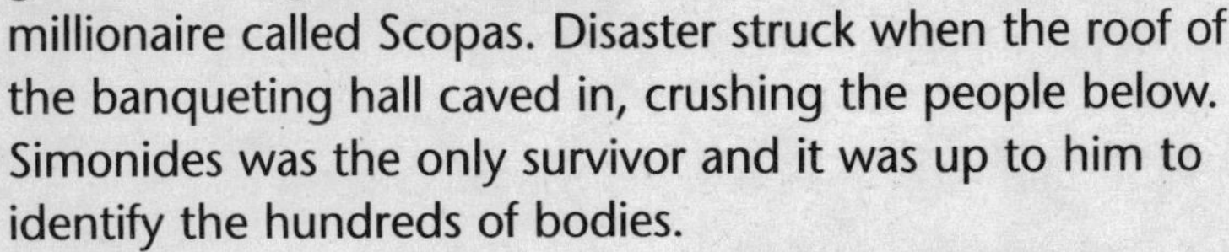

To everyone's amazement, he managed the task with ease. The reason he could do this was that he had trained his memory and could picture the hall full of guests. In his imagination, he could bring the whole scene back to life and identify each of the guests by remembering where they had been sitting.

Working out your own framework

Memory and place are very closely linked. You can make use of this when you're learning by using your imagination to arrange information in different, familiar places.

Here's how the system works. You think of a place you know well – say, a building such as your house or your school. Write down the name of the building and the numbers 1 to 10. Now you have to think up a route around your chosen building. Next to the number 1, write down the starting point of the route. Think about where you would tell someone to start if you were giving directions around this building, and then choose that as your starting point. It might be 'front door', 'entrance hall' or 'gate', for example.

Next to number 2, write down the second stopping place on the route. It could be the first room you come to through the front door, a corridor, or some other landmark.

Where does your journey take you next? Write down the name of the third area in the building next to number 3. Carry on like this until you have a route of 10 areas – a framework that you're familiar with.

The final result

If you chose the house where you live, your list may look like this:

MY HOUSE

1. **front door**
2. **hall**
3. **kitchen**
4. **dining room**
5. **living room**
6. **staircase**
7. **bathroom**
8. **my bedroom**
9. **my sister's bedroom**
10. **the airing cupboard**

Whichever places you've picked, you need to be familiar with them and the route from 1 to 10. Spend a few minutes wandering around the memory framework in your mind. Picture yourself at the first location, then imagine you're walking to the second, then the third, and so on through the whole route.

Using the framework

As soon as you're confident with the mental framework you've chosen, you can put it to use. You're going to use it to memorise the following list of famous characters.

Madonna the Queen Mickey Mouse Superman Robin Hood Frank Bruno Michael Jordan David Beckham Dennis the Menace Michael Jackson

As usual, you need to create some memorable images. Spend a few moments reading through the list and picturing each of the characters in your mind. Bring in as many details as possible. What are they wearing? What are they doing? What are they saying?

Now let your imagination take you to the first place on your route. In the example route, that's the front door. Imagine that **Madonna**, the first character on the list, is standing there. Think of ways to make this image as memorable as possible. Perhaps Madonna is swinging on the door as she records her latest single. You could think of how you'd feel if you *really* opened your front door and found Madonna standing there.

Now, in your mind's eye, move to the second place on your route and picture **the Queen** there. What is she doing in that particular place? What bizarre images can you dream up to remind yourself that she's there?

In the example, the second position is the hall, so you might imagine that a long red carpet has been laid down the hall. Perhaps the Queen is sitting on a lavish throne, with servants lined up all the way along the room. On the other hand, you could make the picture even more bizarre by imagining the Queen on her hands and knees, cleaning the hall!

You might picture **Mickey Mouse** sitting eating cheese from the the fridge in the kitchen, **Superman** setting the dining room table with incredible speed, **Robin Hood** using the living room furniture as targets for his bow-and-arrow practice, and so on.

When you've been right round the route, imagining the relevant person in each one, spend a few minutes checking back through the route and remembering your pictures. Then see if you can remember all 10 characters in order.

More frameworks

Any list of words can be turned into image clues and fixed into your memory framework. Once you're comfortable with one building, try designing a few more. You could think up 10 areas around your school, the local library, your best friend's house, and also use favourite walks, paper rounds, shopping centres – as long as you have 10 clear landmarks and you know the order they come in, you can choose anywhere you like.

Memory frameworks are particularly useful when you're learning for tests and exams. You could design a route specially for each subject or section. You might imagine filling up a museum with images to help you in your history test, or placing reminders for your religion exam around your local place of worship. When the time comes to remember, you simply take a mental journey back round the route and pick up the memorable clues you've left.

Top tip

Never say 'I forgot'. Instead, say 'I didn't remember'. Get into the habit of deciding to remember everything you need. If you don't make a point of learning something, how can you help to recall it when you really need it?

8 Remembering numbers

It's easy enough to think up pictures to remind you of words, but what about numbers? What could you imagine to stand for 6, 2 or 9?

Here are some ideas. Experiment to find out which system suits you best.

The number shape system

In this system you think up a picture based on what a number looks like. Simply look at each digit from 0 to 9 and decide on an image with a similar shape. Whenever you see the digit, you'll imagine the image you've decided on.

0 could be a ball, a hoop or a ring.

1 might be a pen, pencil, needle or pin.

2 could look like a swan or an iron.

3 on its side looks like a mountain range.

4 on its side could be a table.

5 might be a hook.

6 could become a whistle, cannon or bomb.

7 might be a lamp.

8 might suggest a snowman.

9 could be a balloon on a stick or a lollipop.

Using the number images

Once you have a picture to stand for each number, you simply do everything you did to learn a list: group the pictures together and connect them into a story or arrange them around a mental route.

If your best friend Sam's new house number was 29, you might picture a **swan** landing on the roof of the house with a **lollipop** in its beak.

Picture this scene vividly enough and you'll always remember the house number. In your mind's eye you see a large swan landing heavily on the roof of Sam's house with a bright pink lollipop in its beak.

Swan stands for 2. Lollipop stands for 9. So the number of Sam's house is 29.

More number ideas

If the number for the combination lock on your bike was 5438, you might picture yourself using a **hook** to pick up a **table**, then setting it down on top of a **mountain**. It's a snowy mountain and you use the table as a steady base for building a **snowman**.

If you imagine leaning your bike against the snowman, you'll always remember that this strange story contains the combination to your bike lock.

Hook stands for 5
Table stands for 4
Mountain stands for 3
Snowman stands for 8

So the secret combination for your bike lock must be 5438.

What a marvel!

In 1996, at London Zoo, Dominic O'Brien memorised a shuffled pack of playing cards – after looking at them for just 38.29 seconds. That means he was studying each card for around seven-tenths of a second!

Number practice

Spend a few minutes trying out the number shape system. Decide on an image for each digit between 0 and 9, and then use them to create pictures for

> **the number of your locker at school – 19.**
>
> **your friend Emma's birthday in May – 24.**
>
> **the code for your burglar alarm – 7368.**
>
> **your new phone number – 91650.**

Always make sure you know what the pictures are supposed to be reminding you about. Link them to the original information in some way. As soon as you're feeling confident about your number shape images, try to answer the following questions from memory.

- What's the code for your burglar alarm?
- What's the number of your school locker?
- What's your new phone number?
- What day in May is Emma's birthday on?

The number rhyme system

Some people find it easier to remember numbers by basing images on rhymes. All you have to do is decide on words that sound like each of the digits from 0 to 9.

Here are some suggestions:

0 fort
1 bun
2 shoe
3 key
4 door
5 hive
6 stick
7 Heaven
8 plate
9 sign

Now, every time you're faced with a number to learn, you simply change it into these pictures and connect them together in groups or stories, or fix them around mental routes.

Using the system

To remember the date of the Great Fire of London in 1666, you might picture a bun on fire, with three people trying to beat out the flames with sticks.

To remember to go to a party at 7.30, you might imagine the party taking place in Heaven. You need to use a heavy iron key to open the door, which came from an old fort.

The images are Heaven, key and fort. That's 7, 3, 0, so the party must start at 7.30.

It's amazing!

Hiroyuki Goto of Japan has memorised the endless number 'Pi' to 42,195 places. The first 100 digits of Pi are 3.1415926535897932384626433832795028841971693993751058209749445923078164062862089986280348253421170 67.

Mr Goto has memorised that amount 421 times over. If you were to type out the first 42,195 digits in standard-size print, they would stretch 100 metres!

Choose your own rhymes

Choose 10 rhymes of your own for each of the 10 digits. When you're ready to try out the system, have a go at memorising the following information:

Charlie's telephone number is 27318.

You need to meet your Mum at 3.25.

Your membership number at the sports centre is 9460.

Remember to:

- take each digit in turn.
- change it into the word that rhymes with it and picture that word.
- connect the pictures into a scene or story.
- exaggerate the images and involve yourself in the strange goings-on.

When you're ready, see if you can answer the following questions from memory.

When are you due to meet your Mum?

What's Charlie's telephone number?

What's your membership number at the sports centre?

On the bus

Here's a fun memory test to try out yourself – and then use on your friends.

Imagine you're the driver of a bus. At your first stop, five people get on. At the second stop, three people get off and seven get on. Eleven people get on at the third stop. At the fourth stop, eight passengers get off and five get on. When you arrive at the fifth stop, six people get on and 10 get off. Five get off at the sixth stop and two get on. The question is – what's the driver's name?

Answer: Most people are so busy trying to remember all the numbers and keep track of the running total of passengers that they forget the key fact – that you are the driver! The answer is your name.

When you're trying to remember something, it's important to know exactly what you have to remember.

The word length system

The third system is the one you used to memorise the 26-digit number earlier in the book. This is how it works. For every digit you have to learn, you think of a word with that number of letters. That word becomes your picture, ready to be connected with others in your imagination.

With practice, you can pick words that make up appropriate sentences. For example, if the PIN code on your new bank card was 6425, you might think of the phrase 'Please give me money'. Every time you need to remember the number, you simply recall that phrase and turn the words back into digits.

There are six letters in 'please', four letters in 'give', two letters in 'me' and five letters in 'money' – so the PIN code must be 6425.

To remember the digit nought, just include the word 'nought', 'nothing' or 'no' in your memory phrase. For example, you could remember that 6.07 was the time of your train by imagining the guard saying, 'Please – no smoking!'

There are six letters in 'please', the word 'no' stands for nought, and there are seven letters in 'smoking', so your train must be due to leave at 6.07.

Memory marvel

Tibor Rudas is the world's most successful organiser of huge classical music concerts. He created The Three Tenors and was behind the amazing Eiffel Tower concert, part of World Cup '98. In a recent interview, he put down much of his success to his ability to deal with numbers. He said, 'I don't have the patience for things like adding machines and laptop computers. I'm from the old school – everything's in my head, including telephone numbers. While everyone else is multiplying figures and spending time punching numbers into their computers, I've already worked everything out.'

Amazing but true!

Japanese abacus experts get so used to working out mathematical problems on real abacuses that they can do the same thing in their heads. They can visualise the abacus in their mind's eye and use their imagination to help them work out complicated sums. There are contests in which the competitors have to add and subtract up to 15 numbers, each one of between five and nine digits.

Could you do it? Can you work this sum out in your head?

2467023567 + 8765263 + 876287655 + 99812 + 289091 + 7898771 + 987152534 + 879816 + 21652 + 1129387 + 8798723 + 11098889 + 2876512 + 289881

If you can, perhaps you should enter the contests too! (The answer, if you really want to know, is at the top of page 94.)

Brain versus computer

A computer can number-crunch faster than the brain, there's no question about that, and it is a useful tool for some tasks. But never be fooled into thinking that it comes even close to the brain's overall power. You read earlier that computers and brains work differently, and it's that difference that allows you to improve your memory.

As you've discovered, you can use your imagination to fool your memory into thinking that you've smashed a television set or seen turkeys on the Eiffel Tower or built a snowman on top of a mountain. Your brain works through a complicated pattern of interconnections and by making information memorable, you create powerful new connections that will bring it back to you at an amazing speed.

A computer has to trawl mechanically through its data banks but you can use the picture clues you create to access information in split seconds.

(The answer to the sum on page 92 is 4372611553.)

If you asked a computer what Julius Caesar's telephone number was, it would go through all its listings, looking for 'Caesar, Julius'. You, of course, know that Caesar lived way before the telephone was invented so there's no point in even looking!

When there *is* something to be remembered, you can get there by a number of short cuts. If you filled a computer with your personal diary and asked it, 'When did I go to see my favourite band in concert?', it would have to check through the details recorded for every single day. But your mind could find the information in a split second. You might think, 'Why did I go?' It was someone's birthday treat. Whose? Rachel's. Rachel's birthday is 17 September. You would have lots of reminders of the events, and a variety of different brain connections to help you recall the key details required.

It's really not surprising then, that the best chess players in the world still regularly beat the most powerful chess computers. Just being able to carry out millions of calculations a second isn't enough. The human brain knows *which* calculations to do and can approach a puzzle from many different angles.

Amazing but true!

In 1996, World Chess Champion Gary Kasparov beat the program Deep Blue by 4 points to 2 in a match in Philadelphia. Every single second of the match, Deep Blue was looking at 500 million positions!

The man with two brains

The Nobel Prize-winning scientist Roger Sperry discovered that there are two sides to every brain, each doing more of certain kinds of thinking. The right side does more imagining and day-dreaming. It works in pictures and it works in a random way. The left side is much more logical. It likes words, numbers and lists.

A good way to remember the difference is to think of R (right) standing for Random and L (left) standing for Logic.

Professor Sperry discovered that the most effective thinkers use both sides of their brain at once. They think in pictures but also organise their pictures logically.

Using both sides of the brain

Leonardo da Vinci's notebooks still survive and show that he was very imaginative about his inventions, drawing beautiful pictures to illustrate them, and he was also very logical about his art, writing down details about the colours of the paints he wanted to use.

He was imaginative in his logic and logical in his imagination, so no wonder he had an incredible memory and came up with so many amazing ideas and breathtaking works of art.

Leonardo da Vinci was an excellent example of a global thinker. This means someone who thinks with both sides of the brain.

Amazing but true!

Dr Marion Tinsley reigned for 50 years as World Checkers (draughts) Champion. At the age of 65, he played a long match against a Chinook computer program. Chinook had a database containing 27 billion positions, including details of every game Tinsley had ever played. For eight hours a day, five days a week, for two weeks, the two competitors battled it out. Tinsley finally gained victory in the very last game. He leapt out of his seat proclaiming, 'A victory for human beings!'

Test your memory

1 Which chess program did Kasparov beat?

(a) Sky Blue (b) Royal Blue
(c) Light Blue (d) Deep Blue

2 Where did Tibor Rudas organise a concert as part of France '98?

(a) the White House (b) the Great Wall of China
(c) the Taj Mahal (d) the Eiffel Tower

3 What did Roger Sperry win?

(a) the Nobel Prize (b) the Booker Prize
(c) the Turner Prize (d) the George Cross

4 Dr Marion Tinsley was world champion at which game?

(a) draughts (b) chess
(c) dominoes (d) bridge

5 Where did Dominic O'Brien memorise a pack of playing cards?

(a) London Bridge (b) London Zoo
(c) London Airport (d) Tower of London

Answers: 1 (d) 2 (d) 3 (a) 4 (a) 5 (b)

How to remember names

People are always delighted when you remember their names. It shows you're interested in them and it means that they'll probably remember you in future! At school, doing your Saturday job, at parties, always make a point of remembering names. Follow this step-by-step approach and you could remember everyone you meet.

STEP 1 ▶

HEAR THE PERSON'S NAME

It's very easy to be introduced to someone and forget to listen to what that person's called! Two seconds after being told the name, you can't remember it. So always make a point of listening carefully to a person's name.

STEP 2 ▶

BE INTERESTED IN THE NAME

Always spend a few seconds thinking about a name and talk to the person about it if you can. Perhaps it's an unusual name or the same name as a member of your family. How is the name spelt? Give yourself a little time to get to know the name.

STEP 3 THINK UP A PICTURE

What picture does the name suggest? What's the first image that springs to mind?

Sometimes it's obvious. There might be a famous person who has the same name, so you could picture that person. A person's surname might be the name of a job, like Baker, Smith or Butcher, or the name of an object or place that you could picture, such as Ball, Wood, Lake or Bridge.

If no obvious image springs to mind, use your imagination. What does the name sound like or look like? Is there a part of it that might suggest a memorable picture? Here are some examples of picture clues for a few common first names.

Tom	**a tomato**
Amy	**someone taking aim**
Jack	**a jack to raise a car**
Carrie	**a baby's carry-cot**
Adam	**a fig leaf**

Memory marvel

Legend has it that the Persian king, Xerxes, knew the names of all the 100,000 men under his command.

Now you have a go. Think up pictures to remind you of these five names: Mark, Anne, Louis, Beth, James.

Try doing the same with some surnames. Think up some images for the following surnames. (The first three have been done for you, as examples.)

Carter	**a man pushing a heavy cart**
Welsh	**a giant leek**
Roseby	**a bee on a rose**
Carver	**?**
Stonor	**?**
Hillman	**?**
Filgate	**?**
Singh	**?**

Memory marvel

Former US Postmaster James Farley was said to have known 20,000 people by their first names. He described his skill as 'the most effective form of flattery'.

STEP 4 CONNECT THE PICTURE WITH THE PERSON

Whatever strange image you've thought up, now simply picture the person in front of you doing that thing or wearing those clothes or carrying out that job.

You might imagine Mr Carter sitting on his cart to have a rest for a moment. As you speak to Tom, perhaps you picture him squashing a tomato on the end of his nose. When you meet Mrs Roseby, why not think of an angry bee landing on a rose in her buttonhole. Amy Welsh could be aiming her leek at you!

Look for things about the real person you can use as 'hooks' for hanging your images on. What details stand out about this person to make them memorable – and how can you connect them to your images?

Jack's wearing glasses, so perhaps you picture him using a car jack to lift them on and off. Carrie's got long hair, which might prove too much of a temptation to the baby in her carry-cot.

Memory magic

Magicians have often been fascinated by memory tricks. After all, a powerful memory always amazes people and makes them plead with you to tell them how you do it!

Robert Houdin, the great hero of the famous escapologist, Houdini, used to train his memory by playing a kind of Kim's Game (see page 63). He would glance at a shop window for a few seconds, then try to recall every single item he'd seen. David Berglas is the President of the Magic Circle, the number one club for magicians. He has a superb memory and uses it as a basis for many of his tricks.

Harry Lorayne brought memory demonstrations into his magic act and found that they were more popular than his other tricks. He decided to specialise in memory and is now perhaps the most famous 'memory man' in the world. His great skill is remembering people's names. Before a performance, Harry meets as many of the audience members as possible as they file into the theatre. Later, as part of his act, he gets them all to stand up, then sit down again when he points to them and calls out their names.

Harold Parson, Edna McKie, Eric Jones.

It's been estimated that, in his 40-year career, Harry Lorayne has remembered more than eight million names! If you practise the techniques you've learned in this chapter, maybe you can be like him!

Test your memory

1 Name the brilliant king of Persia.

(a) Xerxes
(b) Zenon
(c) Xyno
(d) Zeny

2 What was James Farley's job?

(a) US President
(b) US Postmaster
(c) US Marshall
(d) US Ambassador

3 Which magician trained his memory by playing Kim's Game?

(a) Harbin
(b) Houdin
(c) Copperfield
(d) Houdini

4 What is David Berglas the president of?

(a) The Jockey Club
(b) The Magic Circle
(c) The Kennel Club
(d) The Rotary Club

5 Name the magician who specialises in remembering names.

(a) Henry Latimer
(b) Holly Langridge
(c) Harry Lorayne
(d) Hoby Laughton

Answers: 1 (a) 2 (b) 3 (b) 4 (b) 5 (c)

Memory for exams

One of the big problems when you're trying to remember facts is that you tense up as you try to cram them into your brain and this makes it harder to retain the information you're trying to learn. But tension needn't be a problem if you learn in the most effective way.

Think of how most people approach school tests and exams. They have no memory tricks so they just read through their books a few times, hoping that some of what they are reading will stick in their minds. No wonder they feel nervous when the exam day arrives. They try to hope for the best but really waste huge amounts of mental energy fearing the worst!

If you apply the techniques you've learned in this book to the information you have to memorise, you can be confident that your memory will work. You don't have to waste time and energy worrying about it. You've used your brain in the right way and it will work – so you can enjoy showing off your knowledge!

Techniques for exams

Here's a guide to using mnemonic techniques in exams and tests.

1 GET MOTIVATED

Before you start, remind yourself *why* you're learning. What's in this for you? Give yourself treats and rewards for success.

2 BE CONFIDENT

This is such an important part of the memory process. Don't go around saying you're going to fail, or you might start believing it! Pretend you're an athlete, psyching himself up before a big race. If you've done the right sort of learning, you really can be confident that it's going to pay off.

3 CREATE A MEMORY ZONE

Remember to find a place to work that suits you. Get the location, noise level, furniture and temperature right and you'll give yourself a headstart.

4 ORGANISE

Organise your work by finding out exactly what you have to learn and making sure that you have all the right material to hand. Organise your time by working out a revision plan. How long do you have before the test? How much will you have to do each day to keep on top of the work?

5 WORK IN SHORT BURSTS

Your mind can only concentrate for a while before it starts to get tired. If you try to keep going when you're not taking anything in, you're just wasting your time. Experiment – find out how long you can work well for, and stick to sessions of that length. Many people find that they work best for about half an hour at a time.

6 BREAK TO RELAX

When each short learning session is over, take a break for a few minutes. Do something different to relax. Have a walk, read a book or have something to eat. Don't leave it too long, though, or you might find it hard to get back to work.

7 FOCUS

For every subject you have to revise, ask yourself exactly what it is you have to remember. What are the key things you will need to know to pass the exam? You can often jot down a list of key words that would remind you of details for a history test, say, or a science experiment. Then learn them just like you learned the shopping lists or the items in Granny Went to Market (see page 73).

8 USE YOUR MEMORY

You know how your memory works, and what you've got to do to make it work for you. Break your work into lists of key words, use picture clues to remind you of all the information you need to remember, and connect your pictures together in scenes, stories and routes. Bring in colours, feelings and emotions and take control of all your revision material.

Be imaginative *and* logical. Think globally.

9 WORK WITH A FRIEND

It sometimes helps to link up with a friend who's studying the same subject. Swap learning tips, get your friend to test you, and make sure you test him or her because that's an excellent way of checking that you know your stuff.

10 STAY FIT

There's a Latin expression, *'Mens sana in corpore sano'* which means 'A healthy mind in a healthy body'. A healthy mind needs a healthy body to support it. Get plenty of sleep, eat healthily and take regular exercise, and you'll feel great in body and mind when the day of the exam arrives.

The reason that it is important to stay healthy is that your brain needs various things in order to work properly. It needs to be supplied with oxygen from the body and it needs a number of important nutrients.

World Chess Champion Gary Kasparov trains his body as much as he trains his brain. He runs, swims and lifts weights so that the blood is flowing well to power his memory. I've always found that an exercise session boosts my memory power. When I've tested my success before and after going for a run or playing tennis, I've found that my recall is noticeably better afterwards.

A healthy, varied diet is crucial to good thinking. Try to stay away from too much processed food, fat and sugar, and eat plenty of fruit and vegetables.

Good memory foods

Some foods are believed to be particularly important for memory power. Egg yolks, fish, wheat and soya beans contain lecithin, which is believed to boost memory and learning. Wheat, soya beans, milk and meat contain glutamic acid, another important brain fuel. And there's a substance called phenylalnine in dairy products and meats which is also vital to the learning process.

Fish has often been called 'brain food', and science is now proving this to be the case. Seafood, especially sardines, herrings and anchovies, contains a substance that helps transmit electrical impulses to the brain. Fish also contains ribonucleic acid, which improves memory and increases the life of brain cells.

So help your memory to do its work with good food, regular exercise and plenty of sleep.

Picturing a winner

One of the best things about developing your memory is that it improves your imagination. If you get into the habit of thinking up an image every time you want to learn something, your powers of imagination will become incredibly strong.

Top sportsmen and women use imagination to improve their performance. They picture themselves running the perfect race, throwing the javelin further than ever before, or scoring a spectacular goal, and these positive images help them when they're training and competing.

In their minds, they can focus on the things they're doing wrong, and work out ways of changing them. They can try out new moves in their imagination, practise difficult manoeuvres, and use their memories to motivate them and increase their confidence. They can remember what it feels like to win and use that as a powerful boost to their morale. They can also recall how bad it feels to lose and make sure that they avoid defeat at all costs.

Mental preparation

Top golfer Jack Nicklaus estimates that half of his training is mental preparation. He's spoken about the hours he spends picturing the perfect swing, imagining the feeling he gets when he strikes the ball sweetly and it flies towards the hole.

On the morning before she played in a Wimbledon final, tennis player Virginia Wade spent time just standing on the Centre Court, using her imagination to prepare her for the feelings she would have. She imagined the crowd screaming and clapping, pictured her opponent facing her across the net, and rehearsed her own game in her mind. She saw herself coping with the conditions, playing as well as she could, and winning – and that afternoon she did!

An amazing test

Researchers once worked with a team of basketball players. They split them into three groups. Group A practised every day by throwing real balls into real hoops. Group B did no practice at all. Group C practised throwing the ball in their imagination.

At the end of a week, not surprisingly, Group B had not improved at all. But amazingly, Group C, who had only practised in their imagination, had improved almost as much as Group A. Mental training was very nearly as productive as slogging it out on the real court!

After the experiment, the players resolved to train mentally as well as physically, and the improvement in their overall performance was incredible.

A trained imagination is a very useful tool. Try practising your favourite sports mentally as well as physically. You can use your imagination in this way to prepare for exams as well. In fact, you can use it to help cope with any type of challenge where you need to remember things.

Using the imagination technique

Picture yourself succeeding, coping with difficulties and meeting every challenge, and you'll have a great chance of succeeding for real.

Use your trained memory at every opportunity. Turn all information you have to learn – words, numbers, names, facts – into pictures, and then organise them into scenes, stories or mental routes.

Make it all as vivid as possible, with colours, sounds, tastes and textures.

Involve yourself in the action and make everything as exciting, funny, strange and memorable as you can.

Top tip

Give your memory muscles a workout by going back to your earliest memory. Where were you? Who were you with? What was happening? After working out the broad details, focus on more precise information. Pick a particular sound, taste or smell that comes back to mind and see if it sparks off other memories. Keep working on this event. How many different memory pathways to it can you discover?

How's your memory now?

How much has your memory improved since you started reading this book?

Look back to page 25, where you wrote down your Starting Memory Level. It's time to see if your level has changed.

Take the tests again, scoring yourself exactly as you did before, but using all the memory tricks you've learned in this book. You don't have to take all the tests at once. Give your memory time to rest between each one and note down your scores as you go along.

At the end, count up your marks and work out your new memory level.

Take the tests again in two weeks, then in a month, and keep a record of your progress. Your target is to reach 'Exceptional' status, a score of more than 90 per cent. Be confident. I learned to have a super-power memory and so can you!

An object test

Give yourself five minutes to look at the objects in List A.

LIST A

vase umbrella necklace iron brush bicycle shoe hat pan bottle

Now cover them up and look at List B. Can you underline the ten words from List A?

LIST B

iron chair key scales coat brush box hat vase pen bicycle tie necklace shoe toaster watch umbrella bottle pan book

Check your success. Give yourself two points for each word you recognised.

A word test

You have five minutes to memorise the following list of words.

custard shark car fridge cheese dog hill sand ant cake

(Turn back to page 54 for a reminder of the best method.)

When the time's up, see how many of the words you can write down from memory. You score two points for each one you get right.

A telephone number test

The time limit for this test is 10 minutes. How many of the following phone numbers can you commit to memory?

Dentist	**3298**
Library	**2891**
Restaurant	**9861**
Roller rink	**5034**

(Turn back to page 82 to remind yourself of the number system.)

Cover up the numbers and give yourself five points for each one you get exactly right.

Names and faces

Take a look at these 10 people. You have 10 minutes to learn their names.

(Turn back to page 98 to get some tips on how it's done.)

Now cover them up and look at the pictures below. Can you put the correct names to the 10 faces?

When you've finished, check your success and give yourself a point for every correct first name and a point for every surname you remember.

Characters

Look at these famous names: 10 have been mentioned in this book, and 10 have not. Choose the 10 you think you remember, then check with the answers below. You score two points for every one you get right.

Leonardo da Vinci   Albert Einstein   Placido Domingo

Pele   Sherlock Holmes   William Shakespeare

William Wordsworth   Jane Austen   Michael Faraday

Bobby Fischer   Virginia Wade   Boris Becker

Julius Caesar   Clint Eastwood   Sir Winston Churchill

Samuel Johnson   Florence Nightingale   Jack Nicklaus

Prince Charles   Hercule Poirot

How did you do? Add up the points you scored on each of the five tests to get your final memory level, out of 100.

Less than 10	**Poor**
11-30	**Not bad**
31-50	**Average**
51-70	**Good**
71-90	**Excellent**
More than 90	**Exceptional**

Answers:
Leonardo da Vinci, Albert Einstein, Sherlock Holmes, William Shakespeare, Bobby Fischer, Virginia Wade, Julius Caesar, Sir Winston Churchill, Samuel Johnson, Jack Nicklaus.

Your amazing brain

Right now your brain holds huge stores of information, but there's room for plenty more.

FACT
Your brain already contains enough information to fill an encyclopedia 10 billion pages long!

FACT
You could feed 10 new items into your memory every second for your whole life and it would still be less than half full.

Practice makes perfect

So your brain can do it but remembering is like any other skill. You have to practise to get really good. This book contains all the tricks you need to have a super-power memory. All you have to do now is to put them into practice, wherever you are.

Make a definite resolution to remember

people' names **telephone numbers** **shopping lists**
sporting techniques **recipes** **facts and figures**
birthdays **jokes**

Remember everything now!

Absolutely anything can be given a picture and fixed into place in your mind. Practise your storytelling technique so that you can turn anything into a list of key words and commit it to memory. Practise your favourite number system to learn telephone numbers, codes, prices, times, dates. Practise creating new mental routes around buildings and walks, and fill them with images to remind you of people, facts, books, jokes.

Whenever you have to revise for an exam, make sure you follow all the important rules and turn every collection of information into a list of key words, and that list into a memorable pattern of images. You'll save time, have fun learning, feel more confident, and get much higher marks.

I used to have a *pretty* good memory. Now I never forget anything. I make everything memorable, which is what you have to decide to do today – and keep doing. The results will be incredible.

Good luck – and happy memories.

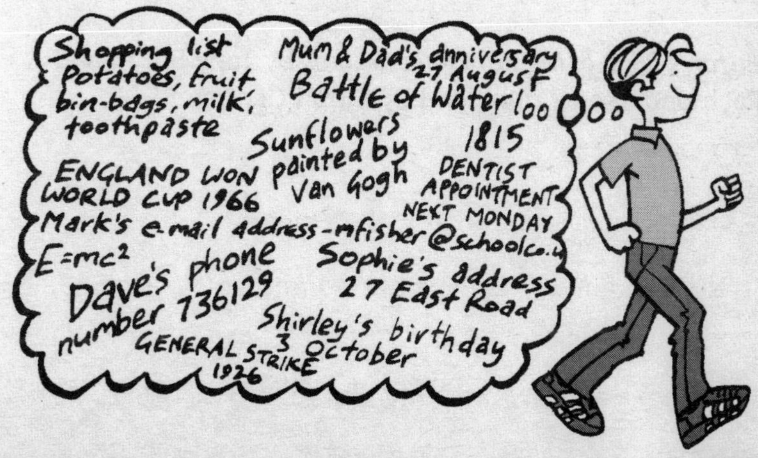

Taking things further

Web sites

For details about memory competitions and the Mind Sports Olympiad:

http://www.mindsports.co.uk/

For more details about global thinking and remembering:

http://www.bdance.com/bdance/homepage.htm

Further reading

Have a Mega Memory by Jonathan Hancock, published by Hodder Children's Books.

Memory by Herbie Brennan, published by Reference Point.

Use your Memory by Tony Buzan, published by BBC Books.

Buzan's Book of Mental World Records by Tony Buzan and Raymond Keene, published by Buzan Centres.

Glossary

cerebellum The part of the brain involved in balance and muscle co-ordination.

cerebral hemisphere The largest part of the brain, involved in thought and memory.

Chinook A powerful computer checkers (draughts) program.

Deep Blue A powerful computer chess program.

global thinking The technique of using both sides of the brain at once.

glutamic acid An amino acid which is important to the memory process. It is found in wholewheat, soya beans, milk and meat.

hologram A three-dimensional picture created by lasers and thought by some scientists to be the best way to understand how the brain stores information.

lecithin Found in egg yolks, fish, wheat and soya beans, lecithin breaks down into a substance which is believed to boost memory.

left brain The part of the brain concerned most with logical thinking, numbers and lists.

medulla oblongata The part of the brain that controls breathing and blood pressure.

mnemonic A memory aid.

neuron A brain cell.

phenylalnine An amino acid found in dairy products and meat. It is important for the memory.

phrenology The study of the shape and size of the head, and the belief that mental processes go on in precisely separated areas.

pi An endless number, often learned to thousands of places by memory performers. Pi measures the ratio of the circumference of a circle to its diameter.

right brain The part of the brain concerned most with random thoughts, pictures and ideas.

ribonucleic acid Found in fish, ribonucliec acid is thought to improve the memory and extend the life of brain cells.

wax table concept A concept invented by the Ancient Greeks, who believed that remembering was like writing on a wax tablet – the memories would always fade with time.

Index

ACTIVATORS

All you need to know

0 340 715162	Astronomy	£3.99	☐
0 340 715197	Ballet	£3.99	☐
0 340 736305	Basketball	£3.99	☐
0 340 715847	Birdwatching	£3.99	☐
0 340 715189	Cartooning	£3.99	☐
0 340 736496	Chess	£3.99	☐
0 340 715200	Computers Unlimited	£3.99	☐
0 340 736275	Cricket	£3.99	☐
0 340 715111	Cycling	£3.99	☐
0 340 715219	Drawing	£3.99	☐
0 340 736313	Film-making	£3.99	☐
0 340 736291	Fishing	£3.99	☐
0 340 715138	Football	£3.99	☐
0 340 736321	In-line Skating	£3.99	☐
0 340 715146	The Internet	£3.99	☐
0 340 736267	Memory Workout	£3.99	☐
0 340 715170	Riding	£3.99	☐
0 340 715235	Skateboarding	£3.99	☐
0 340 71512X	Swimming	£3.99	☐
0 340 73650X	Your Own Website	£3.99	☐

Turn the page to find out how to order these books.

more info • more tips • more fun!

ORDER FORM

Books in the Activators series are available at your local bookshops, or can be ordered direct from the publisher. A complete list of titles is given on the previous page. Just tick the titles you want and complete the details below. Prices and availability are subject to change without prior notice.

Please enclose a cheque or postal order made payable to Bookpoint Ltd, and send to: Hodder Children's Books, Cash Sales Dept, Bookpoint, 39 Milton Park, Abingdon, Oxon OX14 4TD. Email address: orders@bookpoint.co.uk.

If you would prefer to pay by credit card, our call centre team would be delighted to take your order buy telephone. Our direct line is 01235 400414 (lines open 9.00 am – 6.00 pm, Monday to Saturday; 24-hour message answering service). Alternatively you can send a fax on 01235 400454.

Title .... First name .... Surname ....

Address ....

....

....

Daytime tel .... Postcode..................................

If you would prefer to post a credit card order, please complete the following.

Please debit my Visa/Access/Diner's Card/American Express (delete as applicable) card number:

Signature ....

Expiry Date ....

If you would NOT like to receive further information on our products, please tick ☐.